DIGITAL TO DOLLARS

HOW TO GET CLIENTS FAST AND ACHIEVE
UNSTOPABLE GROWTH

BY BARRY SCHIMMEL

www.Microshareintl.com

Copyright 2017 Barry Schimmel

All Rights Reserved. No part of this book may be reproduced in any form or by any means, electronic or mechanical, including photocopying, recording, or by any information storage and retrieval system, without permission in writing from the publisher.

Published by Microshare Intl LLC, S. Barrington, IL

Disclaimer: When addressing financial matters, we've taken every effort to ensure we accurately represent our programs and their ability to improve your life or grow your business. However, there is no guarantee that you will get any results or earn any money using any of our ideas, tools, strategies or recommendations, and we do not purport any "get rich schemes". Nothing in this book is a promise or guarantee of earnings. Your level of success in attaining similar results is dependent upon several factors including your skill, knowledge, ability, dedication, business savvy, network, and financial situation, to name a few. Because these factors differ per individuals, we cannot and do not guarantee your success, income level, or ability to earn revenue. You alone are responsible for your actions and results in life and business. Any forward-looking statements outlined in our book, or any other Microshare Intl materials, are simply our opinion and thus are not guarantees or promises for actual performance. It should be clear to you that by law we make no guarantees that you will achieve any results from our ideas or models presented, and we offer no professional legal, medical, psychological or financial advice. If legal advice or other expert assistance is required, the services of a competent professional should be sought.

SPECIAL OFFER

How to get clients fast start Strategy:

- Free One-On-One Consultation
- Spend 30-40 minutes working together to solve your business problems and create a plan for getting clients fast
- Everyone who applies for a consultation receives a gift

4 WAYS TO REGISTER

Mobile Text
Text to: 58885 your name and email with the keyword **UNSTOPPABLE**

Voice
Call 866-603-3995 PIN # 145611

Web
Visit www.Digitaltodollars.net

QR Code

DEDICATION

This book is dedicated to...

My parents, Burt Schimmel and Sue Hardman, whose guidance throughout my life was everything that was needed. They taught me to work hard, be honest, and follow my dreams.

My wife of nineteen years, Jennifer, has always been an inspiration to me and to our two children, Alec & Elissa. She always gives us unconditional love and support.

Thank you to all my clients for believing in me and making this possible.

ACKNOWLEDGEMENTS

This book couldn't have happened without so many people that I need to thank. First and foremost is my wonderful family. My amazing wife, Jennifer, is the person who inspires me to accomplish so much. Alec and Elissa are my whole life and without them I wouldn't be the person I am.

My CLIENTS who given me the opportunity, time and help to get this book completed.

I am deeply grateful to everyone who stood by us and believed. I thank all in my personal and professional circles who influence me. I thank my editor, Jennifer Schimmel. I especially thank my clients who are using these strategies to achieve unstoppable growth in their businesses.

TABLE OF CONTENTS

Introduction 11
Framework 13
How to use this book 17
Discovering The New mindset 20
Lesson #1: Change your mindset 23
Mindset Case Study 32
Lesson #2: Market Message media 35
MMM Case Study 50
Lesson #3: Leverage your time through automation 53
Automate Your Follow-Up 62
Case Study 62
Lesson #4: Getting Clients Fast 65
Phone Case Study 72
Lesson#5: Getting Clients fast using linkedin & Facebook 75
Lesson #6: Get traffic 83
Conclusion 88
About The Author 89

INTRODUCTION

What strategy will help you get client's fast?

Before we begin, let me tell you why I titled this book *Digital to Dollars*:

- **Digital:** You will learn How to use your digital platform to find clients fast.
- **The economy** has shifted, communication has changed, and we "the people" have changed; therefore, you cannot run your businesses, and your sales and marketing strategy, as if it were still the year 2000.
- **Dollars:** You must make money or you're a hobby. You must have money to pay your bills. The more money you have the more people you can help.

The aim of this book is to provide you with a proven and repeatable method for finding new clients fast. It is my desire to convey a clear and simple step-by-step process for understanding and strategically implementing these sales and marketing tactics, with the result of achieving unstoppable growth.

The underlying belief behind this book is:

The world is changing.

If you don't believe this simple axiom, if you want to run your business as if an extraordinary revolution is not taking place, then this book is not for you.

I am writing for the person who realizes that things are different, but who wants to succeed anyway.

My promise is that this current revolution is not a death sentence for your business. The savvy marketer who understands the demands being placed on current businesses can beat the odds and realize massive growth.

In the pages to come, I will help you change your mindset.   What I truly aim to do is facilitate your personal growth in our changing world.

NOTES

FRAMEWORK

This is a framework I created in 2011 which is still works today.

New FRAMEWORK

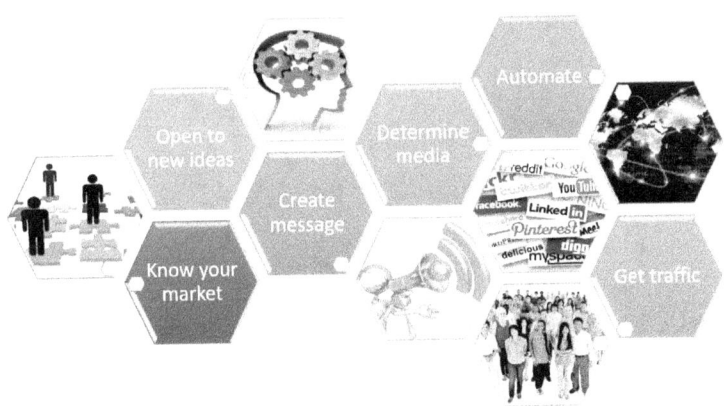

This is a New framework I created in 2017 which is a shortcut. to help you find clients faster.

HOW TO USE THIS BOOK

The first time you read this book, open your mind to new ideas, strategies and tactics. Imagine how you and your business would benefit if you had a pipeline of clients and customers for your products and services.

Ask yourself, what would happen if:

- I had more clients?
- I made more money?
- I had financial freedom?
- I made money while I slept?
- I was known for helping others?
- I could leave a legacy?

There is a second way to use the strategies taught in this book.

When I coach my private clients, my primary goal is give them the path of least resistance.

First, you must look at the problem you solve and who you solve it for. I start by asking questions about their past clients, and then I break them down and analyze the characteristics of the best, and worst ones.

My method is to stop when I know everything about them. Once I've pinpointed their gap, I work with them to fix it. In this way, this framework is one of my most powerful tools for helping businesses grow. And through this book it can be yours as well.

There is one more important thing that I want you to know. Once you discover the gap—the problem—you can systematically work through the framework one strategy at a time, building a solid foundation.

Every time you target a client, your sales and marketing will be more consistent, more effective, and you will get better results.

If you want us to help you with this process, register for a free one-on-one consultation at www.Microshareintl.com

This framework is not a mere tactic, but a way of thinking and executing. And for this reason, you should continually return to this book, take notes, memorize the framework, and…

…Hypothesize, Test and Refine your strategy along the way.

DISCOVERING THE NEW MINDSET

It's vitally important for you to realize that the first step to developing the New mindset is to let go the old one.

Before opening my marketing company—Microshare Intl—in 2010, I had grown three multi-million dollar businesses. Prior to that, I received traditional training while earning my MBA from Roosevelt University in Chicago, IL.

While running my companies, I always knew that it was crucial to keep my finger on the pulse of my marketing. After 25 years, I've learned what works and what doesn't.

In the introduction, I joked about running your business like it is still the year 2000. But in truth, this was a huge hurdle I personally had to overcome. I was very successful during that wonderful decade, and I had mastered the sales and marketing techniques that got results.

I truly wish that the methods that worked then still worked now. It would have saved me hundreds of thousands of dollars, because that is how much it cost me to learn the lessons that are layed out in this book.

There were three important stages that I went through in discovering these lessons.

First, as I already stated, I had to admit that there was a problem (sound familiar?). I realized that the world was changing and that the strategies that I had used to grow businesses before were not working anymore.

Second, I had to have clarity. I learned from the most effective and cutting edge marketers, and I executed countless sales and marketing campaigns.

This book is the culmination of myriad of books read; dozens of trainings, seminars, masterminds and coaching programs; and thousands of mistakes.

In the following sections, I will teach you the Mindset that has taken me many years and a lot of money to learn and refine. You will come away with a framework, a systematic approach, which you can apply time and time again to get results.

LESSON #1: CHANGE YOUR MINDSET

It is essential to change your mindset to change your life.

Myth:

Mindset takes a long time to change, and the longer you have had a belief the more time it takes to revise it. This outdated view goes back to the early days of psychology and neuroscience, when scientists told us erroneously that our brains are hardwired, static and fixed like some sort of machine made purely of physical parts.

What is Mindset?

A set of assumptions, methods, or notations held by one or more people or groups of people that is so established that it creates a powerful incentive within these people or groups to continue to adopt or accept prior behaviors, choices, or tools.

How to change your mindset:

1. **Gather information** about your best clients to understand what problems you solve for them, and who they are. Also, find out what they love and hate and why they love and why they hate.

2. **Analyze** how your competition is converting new leads. The foundation of getting leads is optimizing your message so prospects can understand what problem you solve and your solutions.

3. **Examine your beliefs** about what you are doing and how you are doing it. You must identify what's not working so you can stop doing it and focus on what others are doing that is working effectively.

4. **Create your vision with a clear set of goals** which will shape your mindset to get the results you desire.

5. **Create a message** that is clear, concise and consistent throughout all your platforms.

6. **Protect your mindset** against the naysayers and people who want to drag you down. You also must protect it against poor information and against overload. Keeping your confidence is essential. So please stay on the right path, look to improve yourself and to help others along the way.

Let me clearly explain why mindset is so important. I hear all the time how companies are struggling and digital marketing doesn't work. The biggest complaint I hear is "I have been burned so many times I don't trust anyone"

I can't argue with them because that is their experience. I can help them change their mindset when I follow a proven systematic approach which delivers results.

With this foundational understanding in place, you must evaluate where you are now and where you intend to be a year from now (or even 5 years from now).

The Truth about Mindset

In my marketing firm, Microshare Intl, I have seen many companies grow substantially—in influence and revenue—and it always started with changing the mindset of the business owner. On the flip-side, we have also seen numerous companies fail because they were unwilling to change or did not believe in the new ways to do things. "The difference between success and failure was always in mindset".

Successful companies can change their mindset, in turn influence their marketing and sales actives; unsuccessful companies don't. This is true in every industry.

Change the World and Make Money

In my experience, all businesses function for two reasons:

1. To fulfill a mission (think Mission Statement)
2. To generate revenues

Most companies try to accomplish both, but in varying degrees. As a generalization, not-for-profit organizations lean towards trying to fulfill a Mission, where small and medium size companies (which include Authors, Speakers and Entrepreneurs) focus on revenues.

Here are some great questions that I love to ask my clients, and sadly most of them don't have answer for them:

- What do you love about your business?
- What legacy do you want to leave?
- What have you done in the past toward that legacy?
- What is your company's Higher Purpose?
  (For example, the online shoe store Zappos says, "We are all part of something great… To put a smile upon your face.")

Now that we have concluded mindset, I want to continue forward using the information we gathered from our clients and competition.

6 Steps that will help you change your **Mindset**.

1. Gather information
2. Analyze
3. Examine your beliefs
4. Create your vision with a clear set of goals
5. Create a message
6. Protect your mindset

Sign up at
www.Digitaltodollars.net
for a video that will guide you through these
6 Steps.

MINDSET CASE STUDY

Kris, a chiropractor, was building a very successful practice.

I worked one-on-one with her and went through the six steps to help her change her mindset.

During this time, Kris had a few "aha" moments.

She realized:

1. Who she loved to work with
2. Who she didn't want to work with
3. What she loved to do

I started by helping Kris solidify her unique value proposition and communicating her unique story. She needed to own and convey what set her apart from all the other chiropractors.

In the end, Kris decided to focus on the practice area she loves, which is functional medicine. She is rebranding herself and adding new products and services to her new practice.

I built a graphical framework to illustrate her services and define exactly what problems she solves.

Next, I helped her create a clear, concise message so we could target the patients she desired.

Part of this process was setting up a new website and measurable goals for prospecting.

THE RESULTS

Did Kris's new mindset have any impact?

Over the course of a month, Kris approached 18 prospects and 15 of them agreed to meet for a one-on-one consultation.

The result was 12 new clients... SUCCESS!

LESSON #2: MARKET MESSAGE MEDIA

Know your Market first so you can create the best Message on the right Media.

"Without a solid foundation, you'll have trouble creating anything of value."

- Erica Oppenheimer

Market

Target Market is the market a company wants to sell its products and services to, and it includes a targeted set of customers for whom it directs its marketing efforts. A target market can be separated from the market by geography, buying power, demographics and psychographics.

Where should you start?

1. MARKET
2. MESSAGE
3. MEDIA

This is the first question I always ask prospects.

Where do you start? Market, Message or Media?

95% of people answer this incorrectly.

85% answer Message and 10% say Media.

The most important element for any successful marketing campaign is understanding who you are selling to and what problem are you solving. Which leaves Market as the correct answer.

Remember from lesson #1, gather information from your best client, analyze the competition.

Good communication skills are at the cornerstone of creating results since so much of your relationship with your client has to do with what you communicate, and not just what you do behind the scenes.

Listening is an art, after all, and not everyone knows how to do it properly. If you can master the art of listening, you'll improve your relationships by connecting with a deeper level of understanding.

Remember, your clients care about the problem you are solving for them and will even share other problems they have that you might be able to solve. Keep the communication open, but focus on the right questions.

- **Who are you selling to?**

    Demographics: Gender, education, profession, income, home ownership, geographic location, family, lifestyle, online activity, ideal qualities, and nightmare qualities?

- **What makes them want to buy?**

    Psychographics: Their wants, their innermost fears and frustrations, their objections to buying, and what would make them buy.

- **Do they have money?**

    Another big mistake I see is companies that are failing, are spending their time and marketing dollars on a target audience that doesn't have the ability to pay for their product and services.

In summary, your upfront research in defining your target audience will save you time, money and reduce your stress considerably. Knowing your target audience is the first step to achieving success!

Message

Message is a verbal, written, or recorded communication sent to or left for a recipient who cannot be contacted directly. Your message should be targeted at your target audience while solving one problem at a time.

Ask yourself:

- How will my message bring in new clients?
- How can my message increase conversions?
- How can my message increase the amount I sell to my current clients?
- How can my message help my clients?
- How can my message increase my authority?
- How can my message support my 5-star reputation?
- How will my message integrate with my marketing automation?

Steps to creating your marketing message

We have already identified our target market and the problems they have. The next step is to present your product or service as a simple solution to fix their problem.

Continuing the process, the next step is to present the results you've produced for other clients in the same situation. It's not enough just to tell people you have a solution; you must prove to them that your solution works. Realize, you can talk all day about how you solved this and that problem, but people are skeptical and won't automatically believe you.

People will believe other people who are like them that have achieved positive results. In this step, you'll need to prove your results by providing testimonials from current and former customers as well as case studies of actual problems that were solved and the results that were achieved.

Therefore, your message, has two functions:

- To leave a great first impression
- And to move prospects through the sales cycle

Last, you must explain what makes you different from your competitors. You need to communicate your uniqueness!

Prospects are looking for you to communicate your differences. And those differences need to have perceived value to the prospect. It needs to be something relevant and what they care about.

The Big Marketing Message Mistake

The biggest marketing message mistake that companies make is communicating "What-We-Do" instead of "What's-In-It-For-Me." If these were two radio channels (i.e. WWD vs. WIIFM), which one do you think your prospect would rather hear?

While you are transmitting on WWD, your prospect is looking for the WIIFM station. In order for your message to match your market, you need to be broadcasting on WIIFM.

Creating your Message:
1. Know your market
2. Identify problems
3. Present your solution
4. Present results (posted from current clients for credibility)
5. Explain what makes you different

Sign up at
www.digitaltodollars.net
for a video that will guide you through Creating a message that gets results.

Media

Media is the means of communication - radio and television, newspapers, magazines, and the Internet - that reach or influence people widely:

There are 3 types of media

- Paid Media

    Paid media is what most people think of when they think of advertising. It's the most traditional of the three types of digital media—you pay to leverage an existing channel. Examples include digital display ads, paid search, and native advertising. Paid media lets you reach a large-scale audience and direct attention to your content to those that wouldn't otherwise find it. For example, if you don't rank on the first page of Google for an important keyword, buying an AdWords ad for that keyword will get you views that you couldn't get organically. The downside of paid media is that audiences are bombarded with ads in almost every sphere of their lives, and seeing another ad might not elicit a strong response from them. But if used correctly, it can be a great way to draw in new customers to your content. The goal of using paid media is for the value of this access to dramatically outweigh the cost in dollars of the ad or promotion.

- Earned Media

Earned media is often referred to as "online word of mouth." It includes SEO rankings, social media mentions, and content getting picked up by a third party. In effect, your customers become your promotion channel. Earned media is free, acquired by good strategic practices on social media and SEO, as well as good PR practices. You can't buy someone's good opinion online, which is why this is known as "earned" media—you must work for it. It can be immensely effective because of its organic nature. It's also more credible than a paid ad—more people will listen to a real person's endorsement. Earned media can be problematic because you don't control it, and sometimes your stakeholders have negative opinions of your service. However, word of mouth is a key sales driver, so cultivating earned media is extremely worthwhile. How can my message increase the amount I sell to my prospects and current clients?

- Owned Media

Owned media is perhaps the least understood of the three types of digital media. It's any media that is controlled directly by your brand, such as your company website, blog, or social media account. Everything that you publish on this channel is yours, and you can adapt or change content as you need. Promoting your company on your Twitter account costs far less than promoting it with an AdWords ad.

Owned media builds off your existing relationships with customers as well as drawing in prospects who are further along in the decision-making process. When your audience interacts with your owned media properties, they're often drawn to explore more of your content—if someone likes a blog post on your website, he might click around and view your company capabilities.

Owned media also has the benefit of longevity. Advertisements will only run for so long, but your website will continue to draw in customers as long as it's active and updated. The downside is that there are no guarantees. You could be creating high-quality, well-branded content, and only have a few people view your site each week.

These three types of digital media each have their advantages and disadvantages, which is why they shouldn't be used in isolation from each other.

Our goal is to determine where our clients are hanging out, and target our messaging at the right place and right time to get them interested in our products and services.

MMM CASE STUDY

A local printing company, we'll call them The Print Guy, was expanding their operation. They knew their business very well, but wanted me to consult with them on Marketing Strategy to ensure their marketing continued to be suitable for their quickly expanding business.

After our initial consultation, I continued working through the framework. It was time for a website that started a conversation with The Print Guy's best client.

We integrated the findings from our extensive strategic research with the "Steps for creating a message".

We crafted a video script for the The Print Guy's CEO for the front page of their website. This video used copywriting best-practices to engage the viewer and persuade prospects to use The Print Guy's services. The video also established credibility and introduced the brand.

We added value to the visiting prospects by creating an irresistible foot-in-the-door-offer and gave it away for free. In turn, the prospects supplied us with their name and email (lead capture). By delivering this valuable free offer, we positioned the printing company as an authority and elicited reciprocity. Most importantly, through this exchange of content for their email, our client now had permission to continue marketing to these prospects (list building).

Next, it was very important to give the prospect the experience of being "your customer through your current clients." Therefore, we videotaped customer testimonials and posted current reviews on the front page of their website (Credibility).

The Results

Now for the real test....

We trained the sales people and office staff at The Print Guy's to direct prospects to the website and watch the videos and read all the 5-star reviews.

The outcome: Sales increased and the sales cycle was shortened.

...Success!

LESSON #3: LEVERAGE YOUR TIME THROUGH AUTOMATION

Leverage is an awesome force–it allows us to multiply our abilities by applying a little pressure to something.

Technology: an evil temptress for productivity…

Technology can suck us in with promises of simple task management, planning, and keeping us in the loop. Unfortunately, we can easily get caught in the vortex of more, more, and more tech. Use a simple task manager if it suits your work style, but give yourself limits on social networking sites, checking email, and even text messaging (if that's your thing).

Ironically, there are really cool apps and software packages that help increase your productivity, so be careful and mindful of how you're leveraging your time.

The New Paradigm: Marketing Automation

Wouldn't it be great if you were able to follow-up and get business from everyone that visited your website or that you met at a networking event or tradeshow?

What are you doing with all the business cards you have collected that is easily manageable?

How would your business be impacted if you were giving your best presentation to each and every prospect you met either in person or as they visited your website?

This principle of Automating Your Follow Up puts your online marketing concept on steroids. It also optimizes how you leverage your time.

If you're running even a nearly-decent company, you have at least three burning lessons, principles, or facts that you wish you could teach to every single prospect and client that you have. The truth is that you just don't have time to sit with people one-on-one and educate them.

Are you tired of saying the same thing over and over and over again? Are you sick of working so darn hard to build relationships?

Introducing Marketing Automation!

Cross Channel Marketing Automation allows you to take your online content and digital information and make it easily accessible to anyone you engage with. This is expansive... networking events, tradeshows, speaking engagements, and business meetings. This list is endless.

It allows you to record your absolute best presentations and deliver them to your targeted clients while you sleep. More importantly, it allows you to deliver your messages in whatever way your prospects respond best (Email, Text, Voice, Audio, Video, etc.). If you can conceive it, then it can be automated.

Imagine someone watching your video on a smart TV while lying on the couch. Traditionally, you would end with a call to action that invites them to your website. But, what if they could simply take out their cell phone and text in to receive your valuable and informative content?

Or imagine that you are coming home from a tradeshow with dozens of business cards... What if you could use a mobile app to scan these business cards straight into your database—with permission of course—and automatically (or as a client of mine says 'like magic') send an informative PDF and video business card which contains video testimonials right to their inbox?

Value, Value, Value, Sell

If this seems complicated, let me simplify it for you.

Using technology, you can save time, provide useful solutions, and make more money.

Here's the core concept behind Marketing Automation. When you sell, you cannot follow up with everyone the required sixteen times that it takes to close the average sale. So, you are using your discretion to decide who to engage with.

The challenge is that even the absolute best salespeople are wrong a good percentage of the time. With marketing automation, I close many prospects who are not on my Hot-List and even clients who I haven't spoken to in months. Many of these people definitely would have slipped through the cracks if I didn't Automate my Follow Up.

Here's how it works...

When I meet someone, I put them in my system. When people go onto my website, I encourage them to get information that will solve their problem. When I engage on social media I encourage people to opt-in to get information that's solves their problem. In this way, everyone who expresses a genuine interest in my solutions gets funneled into my follow-up sequence.

Here's the secret: I don't sell them anything. Right away, I deliver value first to my prospects. I send them Case Studies, eBooks, Emails that educate, Press Releases, Videos, etc.

I give them something of great value before I ever ask them to buy something from me. I show them Results in Advance.

The key is that all of this takes only 3 seconds of my time. Once I've set up my automated follow-up, all I have to do is enter prospects into my system—always with their permission.

Warning

Now remember that Automated Follow Up is only a conversion tool. If you have a hot prospect who is ready to move forward, simply schedule an appointment and close them. Meet people where they are and pay attention to what they are telling you.

The point of automating your follow up is to increase your conversions by 50%, or even more. It will never replace the process of one-on-one selling, but it does make it significantly easier and more effective.

Getting Started

There are many Automated Marketing tools and strategies. I recommend that you schedule appropriate time to plan your Automated Marketing in your Marketing Strategy Session, or consult with a Marketing Expert.

Here is a list of 10 Marketing Methods. Make sure that the tools you choose are effective for the strategy you chose to go to market. Also, know how your prospects like to communicate.

(See the **10 Vital Cross Channel Marketing Methods** on the next page).

10 Vital
Cross Channel Marketing Methods.

1. Text Messaging
2. Email Auto Responders
3. Web Forms
4. Mobile Kiosk
5. Business Card Scanning
6. Voicemail Marketing
7. Livecasting (Facebook Live)
8. Social Profile Gathering
9. Live Teleseminars and Webinars
10. Email Broadcasting

Sign up at
www.MicroshareIntl.com
for more information on how to use cross channel marketing to grow your business.

AUTOMATE YOUR FOLLOW-UP CASE STUDY

An office cleaning company with a small sales force was struggling with consistently following up with prospects.

When we first met with the owner, Anthony, he complained that his staff seemed to be too late to get the sale. Too many times his team would follow up with prospects just days after they had already switched to a new cleaning company. It was an issue of time and timing. His salespeople just couldn't follow up enough to retain top of mind awareness. Because of this, many opportunities were lost.

We walked the team through Rules 1 to 5, then created a follow-up sequence to automate their best sales presentations.

The first step was to gather all of their marketing material and make sure they had a clear, concise message with a call to action.

Next, we videotaped Anthony presenting the company's unique story, irresistible offer, and an overview of their services. Prospects could now experience the benefit of hearing and seeing their best presentation and getting to know, like and trust the company.

The sales people would meet a prospect and enter the prospect's name and email into a web form right from their phone or company website and the prospect would immediately be in the sales funnel.

A couple times a month, the prospect would receive high quality content from Anthony and team. His cleaning company was now front and center in the prospect's mind. When the prospect was ready to proceed, he had current information from the cleaning company and their contact information at his fingertips. (Top-of-mind awareness).

The Results

The funnel was filled was built from scratch, filled with people who are already proven buyers for their product.

This synergistic relationship between you and automated tools will help keep prospects moving through the sales process until they are ready to work with you.

Follow-up was no longer an issue and Anthony's frustrations were solved.

...Success!

LESSON #4: GETTING CLIENTS FAST

The truth is you need more clients now or else!

Attitude

First, set your attitude toward success by doing three things:

- Be bold. Don't take anyone's advice about not doing something that will make people pay attention to you (as long as it's legal, of course).

- Be creative. Startup time is your most creative. In fact, when business owners who've been around awhile ask me what they can do to add new zest to their businesses, I ask them to tell me what they did when they first launched-and do it again.

- Give up your fears, doubts and insecurities. You'll love yourself better when you do and experience freedom!

Next, take massive action:

Take out your phone

This is where **Digital to Dolla**rs starts to "**Get you Clients Fast!**"

Are you frustrated with all the marketing you've implemented because you don't get the results you desire?

Well, I'm here to tell you that all the blog and social media posts you have actually do help. Now you need to take your efforts to the next level. Let's start with your phone. I am going to take you through some strategies I use every day that have given me access to opportunities I would have never thought to pursue.

First, look at each contact on your phone and think about why they are there. Find all the people that you have talked to, that you should be calling to offer your solution to solve their problem.

Next, think about the conversation you had with them and try to do one or all the following:

1. Call
2. Text
3. Send SMS (Video)

Here is how my conversation starts when I first meet someone.

Hello, I'm Barry Schimmel with MicroShare and they reply I'm Joe Prospect. What do you do for a living Barry? I say, if you don't mind I like to hear what you do so I can answer your question in a way that serves you. They go on to tell me what they do and I ask a few questions:

- How do you market your products or services?
- Is that working for you?
- What works best?
- What has been one of your biggest challenges?

Now I can answer what I do:

I help business just like yours get clients fast by helping you overcome _____ *(State Biggest Challenge).* Now only be authentic, moral and ethical. This is not to be used to con someone.

If you feel comfortable, take a picture with them and add them to your contacts. I normally ask for their cell number and text them the picture of us so they can remember who I am.

When I get home, I shoot a 20 second video and wait one day to follow up. The video goes like this: "Great meeting you at ____ *(The Event).* I have a couple of ideas that will help you overcome ____ *(the challenge they mentioned).* Do you have anytime to meet next week?

Now you can always send a text and attach the picture you took with them so they absolutely remember who you are.

The same idea will work if you are following up with old contacts. I do research first to understand who they are and what they do currently. I also look at their competition so I understand what challenges they might have before I contact them.

Think about how you can implement this type of strategy for your business!

Six Ways to use your phone to get new clients:

1. Call old contacts
2. Text old contacts
3. Send SMS Video
4. Take picture with prospect
5. Send them the picture (capture cell #)
6. Follow up

Sign up at
www.Digitaltodollars.net
for a video that will guide you through choosing the best way for you to use your phone.

PHONE CASE STUDY

Diane, who is a tax consultant, was sitting near me at an event and my introduction was exactly as I stated above.

Her biggest challenge was online conversions.

I asked her if we could take a picture together and I would text it to her so she would remember who I am. (If you do not see an opportunity to help the prospect, I do not recommend doing this).

Next, I researched her business and her competition and figured out how I could serve her business.

I then strategically shot a 20 second video and attached it to the text.

"This is Barry, check out this short video."

She texted me back and asked to setup a consultation! Next, we connected on LinkedIn and I could see that Diane viewed my profile and was doing her research on me.

The Results

We had our meeting!

The end result was a new client.

...Success!

LESSON #5: GETTING CLIENTS FAST USING LINKEDIN & FACEBOOK

LinkedIn taps into the power of LinkedIn's 450M+ member network to help Sales professionals find and build relationships with prospects and customers through social selling.

As of the third quarter of 2016, Facebook had 1.79 billion monthly active users. In the third quarter of 2012, the number of active Facebook users had surpassed 1 billion. Active users are those which have logged in to Facebook during the last 30 days.

I hear from many small businesses that they are ready to shut the doors because they can't find enough business.

Well, all I must say is the economy has shifted and the old ways of doing sales and marketing isn't working. Over the last year, I felt the shift, the pressure and the flow of leads decrease. Then I woke up and changed what I was doing. I put my beliefs aside and started testing different ways of communicating and different platforms to incorporate.

I never thought I would use direct messaging on LinkedIn and Messenger on Facebook

The truth is that you must go where your clients and prospects are hanging out whether you like it or not, if you want to get their attention.

How can I get my prospects' attention?

In the introduction, I asked you to open your mind and change your mindset.

Then I asked you to research your market, message and media.

Now, I want you to look at how you can find your ideal client on LinkedIn and Facebook.

I know – "Your target market doesn't go on Facebook." I hear it all the time, but you just read the statistics. With that limiting belief, you'll let your competition steal the opportunities away from you while the rest of us reach, help and serve others.

First, I want to share a strategy I used, and if your connected to me on LinkedIn, you might have seen my email if you fit my target audience.

I viewed 100 profiles each day and sent a message through LinkedIn. Yes, the free version.

It went like this:

Hello Bret, Can I send you clients?

I am reaching out to you today because I feel your business is a good fit for me to send you clients.

My name is Barry Schimmel and I have helped 48 companies this year, just like yours get a steady stream of qualified leads using my "7 Step Systematic Approach".

I know what you might be thinking - that your business is different.

I agree.

That why I would like you to set aside about 20 minutes of your time to talk, and as an ethical bribe, I will give you a copy of my Amazon #1 Best Seller "7 New Marking Rules" for free. I will send it directly to you after our call, no strings attached. I promise, I will make good use of your time as I know it's valuable. If you feel the time is right, email me your best number with a couple of dates and times you are available or call me at 847-304-7885.

Over the course of 4 days, I sent 400 messages like this out and made 37 appointment and closed over $30,400 in business.

How's that for never using LinkedIn to prospect before? The real challenge is handling all the responses and setting up meetings.

If you think it was a fluke, I have another quick story. I belong to a community of marketers and I got a call asking for help as everything he was doing was not working and his wife wanted him to go find a job.

I told him to try this same strategy, and within a couple of days, he was setting up appointments. Now, he has one opportunity that is starting out at $15,500 and has the potential to be worth over $200,000.

Not bad for a few hours of cutting and pasting some text.

This is the power of Digital!

Facebook Live

What is it? It is a way to use your phone to broadcast your video over the internet live.

Have engaging conversations with your followers.

Live is the best way to interact with viewers in real time. Field their burning questions, hear what's on their mind and check out their Live Reactions to gauge how your broadcast is going.

I use Facebook Live as part of my strategy to let people know what I'm up to and really educate them on what I do and how I do it, without any selling.

You can reach new audiences in new ways.

People love watching videos, which is why they built a dedicated place to watch this engaging content on Facebook. While your current fans will be able to keep up here and in Newsfeed, the experience will help new followers discover you too.

Live helps you Connect instantly.

Live lets you connect with the people who care most. Your followers can receive notifications when you go live so they know to tune in to your broadcasts at just the right time.

Three Essential Facts

1. Prospects are on LinkedIn.

2. Prospects are on Facebook.

3. Yes, you can be too.

Sign up at
www.MicroshareIntl.com
for a free consultation on how you can target your message on free platforms

LESSON #6: GET TRAFFIC

You would be rich if everyone who meets you for the first time buys from you.

Creating Your Profit Machine

How come are so many people making money online and I don't?

Great question. I am really excited to talk to you about this very subject. I have spent tens of thousands of dollars to find out there is no way to get rich quick. Sorry!!!

There is a way is take a short cut:

Work with a coach that can help you eliminate most of the mistakes you are going to make along the way.

You can also take courses and do it yourself. I will admit after a decade of doing this myself, I recommend you focus on what you do best and let the experts focus on what they do best.

What I want to show you is one of the fastest ways to sell your products and services and even make money while you sleep.

1. Create a live webinar

   You first have to create your presentation which clearly defines who you are, what problem you solve, and who you solve it for. Now, give examples of people you have helped. Where were they before you and where are they today because of you.

2. Create a **Call to Action** in your webinar which lets the prospect purchase what you are selling or sign-up for a free consultation. You can automate this process with appointment setting software such as Schedule Once, Appointlet, Timetrade etc.

3. Use Facebook Ads

   Our goal is to attract prospects most likely to buy. Want to know the first rule of marketing? Sell what people want! Craft the perfect message that sells every time.

   Here's how simple the flow goes for a product or service. There will be times where you can even get the sale before the webinar.

   Facebook Ad → Webinar → Consultation

4. Automate the webinar

   The key here is to make sure you have a chat role that look live and if possible you have some that can answer questions. Prospects will stay on longer if they think its live.

3 Steps to Getting Clients Fast!

1. Create a live webinar
2. Create a clear call to action
3. Use Facebook Ads
4. Automate the webinar

Sign up at
www.MicroshareIntl.com
for more information on how to use
this method setup a consultation.

CONCLUSION

Congratulations! By finishing this book, you have completed "How to get clients fast and achieve unstoppable growth." If you are a currently marketer, you now know more about marketing in the New World than 90% of your peers. If you are a business owner, you probably know more than 99% of your competition.

It is time to first celebrate your victory. You created a goal of finishing this book, and now you have accomplished it. As I teach in my book ***Success Junkie***, it is very important to take time, even if it can only be a moment, to celebrate your victories. Recognize that you are one step closer to reaching your Vision and be joyous. Know that I am proud of your success and very grateful that you took the time to listen to my teachings.

Your next step is to nurture these lessons and then take massive action!

ABOUT THE AUTHOR

Barry Schimmel has been an entrepreneur for over 25 years and has founded three multi-million dollar companies.

His client experience is deep and includes Pepsi Cola Bottling Co., American Express, and Temple Inland, among many other Authors, Speakers and Entrepreneurs.

- Barry earned his MBA in Marketing at Roosevelt University and is a veteran of the United States Airforce.
- He is a member of America's Premier Experts, the Experts Industry Association, and Engaging Speakers.
- He sits on the Board of Directors for the Barrington Area Chamber of Commerce.
- Has been seen on ABC, CBS, NBC and Fox.

In 2010, Barry began teaching what he describes as "the lessons learned through the millions of mistakes along the way." He has inspired thousands across the United States.

To your outrageous success!

OTHER BOOKS BY BARRY

7 New Marketing Rules reached the Amazon #1 Best Seller list, the Amazon Hot New Releases List, and the Amazon Top Rated List.

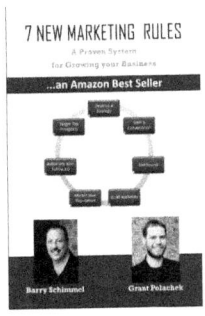

***Success Junkie*: 12 Principles for Winning the Life of your Dreams**

COMING SOON

BARRY CURRENTLY SPEAKS ON...

- The 7 New Marketing Rules
- How to create an income stream that make you money while you sleep
- Cutting Edge Marketing Strategy
- Book Creation and Marketing for Authors, Experts, Speakers and Consultants
- How to get clients fast
- How to get speaking gigs fast
- Creating Celebrity
- Marketing Automation
- Lead Generation

"I picked up new ideas everyone should have, no matter how big or small their company."

- Hazel Wagner,
  www.HazelWagner.com Former instructor, Kellogg Graduate School of Management

"This must-read book highlights the importance of communication in bridging the organization's strategies and goals with their market, message and media. These are the keys to making things happen and getting results."

- Philip Claps
  Founder of KC Printing
  www.kcprint.com

"Barry continues to give and give. The lessons I've learned are invaluable. I am implementing these strategies as you read his book!"

- Andrea Herran,
  Owner of Focus HR
  www.FocusHR.biz

"Barry has proven track record of helping Speakers grow their business by implementing these simple, but brilliant strategies. I highly recommend his book!

- Gail Brown
  Co-Founder of Engaging Speakers
  www.EngagingSpeakers.com

"I'm already seeing results and I'm only half-way through the book."

- Mark Papadas
  Founder of I am 4 Kids Foundation
  www.IAm4KidsFoundation.org

"What a powerful resource!!! These strategies deliver results and they are easy to implement and cost effective for any business. I wish I knew these strategies sooner!"

- Mike Imm
  Barrington Allstate Agent
  agents.allstate.com/michael-imm-barrington-il.html

"Barry Schimmel has developed proven, thoughtful marketing methodologies that help businesses succeed in their everyday efforts. Like a football coach calling a play based on game conditions, Barry's vision and tools ensures companies use the right message at the right time with the right audience clearly and consistently. Following his mindmaps gives you the building blocks and roadmap necessary to win in today's business environment."

- Michele Malo
  Entrepreneur, Speaker, Personal Trainer.
  www.wc-h.com

NOTES

www.ingramcontent.com/pod-product-compliance
Lightning Source LLC
Chambersburg PA
CBHW070719210526
45170CB00021B/698